Praise for Will Nixon's Previous Poetry Book
My Late Mother as a Ruffed Grouse

"Will Nixon's narrative poems strike a rare balance between a child's sense of wonder and a skeptic's dry, knowing assessment of the world. Whether we leap with him from a mountaintop, fight World War I in his basement, or accompany him as he wakes up 'under blue lights buzzing like patio zappers/ in the emergency hall beside a mummy face/ with more tubes up its nose than a distributor cap,' we know at every wrenching turn or droll digression that we're in the presence of a born storyteller."

--Mikhail Horowitz, *Rafting into the Afterlife*

"Nixon's autobiographical-feeling narratives touch more lives than his own: the first crush on a teacher, the scavenging lust of urban bohemians, the Catskill walkabouts, the difficult deaths of two parents. His language is clean and startling."

--*Chronogram*

"From boy to teen to young newlywed, from suburbs to city to ultimately a mountain lifestyle that somehow suits the poet as well as oxygen, we have seen firsthand the evolution and maturing of one human being. The transformation hasn't been accomplished without error, and the poems don't try to hide mistakes made along the way. It's a nostalgia tale told with compassion and without apology."

--*Home Planet News*

"Will Nixon's *My Late Mother as a Ruffed Grouse* is packed with intelligent, entertaining poems that are full of life, poems that you will want to read again and again for the pure enjoyment, as I have."

--Matthew J. Spireng, *Young Farmer, Out of Body, Encounters*

"Just what satisfying poetry should be: rich in metaphor and surprise."

--Bobbie Katz, *The Monsterologist, Once Around the Sun, We the People*

Now in its Second Printing

Love in the City of Grudges

Will Nixon

FootHills Publishing

Acknowledgments

Some poems in this collection have appeared, often in earlier versions, in the following journals: *American Jones Building & Maintenance, Amoskeag, &, Bellowing Ark, Borderlands: The Texas Poetry Review, The Broome Review, Confrontation, The Country and Abroad, Diner, The Front Range Review, Green Hills Literary Lantern, Hawai'i Pacific Review, The Higginsville Reader, Hunger, Iconoclast, Main Street Rag, Mobius, Naugatuck River Review, Prima Materia, Rockhurst Review, Slipstream, Stained Sheets, Tar River Poetry, Wisconsin Review, The Worchester Review, Xanadu.*

The Hudson Valley Writer's Guild awarded "The Prophet of Protrero Hill" second place in its 2009 poetry competition.

The Upper Delaware Writers Collective's Green Heron Poetry Project published "Saying Cheese, 1960" as a poster.

"Mother Reanimated" appeared in *Vanguard Voices of the Hudson Valley Poetry 2007* published by the Mohonk Mountain Stage Company.

"Procrastination" appeared in a different version in *Out of Our Minds: A Collection of Works by Writers in the Mountains.*

"The Leak" appeared in another version in the chapbook *The Fish Are Laughing.*

Cover art by Carol Zaloom

ISBN: 978-0-941053-36-5

FootHills Publishing
P. O. Box 68
Kanona, NY 14856
www.foothillspublishing.com

To My Muses
Thanatos & Eros

Contents

Dog City

Meryl Streep Has Brought All Her Pigeons: Poems of Hoboken in the 1980s

I Feed Her My Heart She Never Stops Eating: Poems Inspired by *Night of the Living Dead*

Dog City

Saying Cheese, 1960

Posed for the Brownie: Tyrolean shorts and dimpled knees,
red sneakers, corn silk hair, thumb held ready
for sucking after the shot. Behind me, scene of my crimes:
our brick apartment with its struggling hedge.
Launched my water rocket into the eye of a crow,
painted a kiss on the Doberman with my mother's lipstick,
bounced my Superball so high it scared an airplane.
Punished, hid inside my wooden toy chest and plotted revenge
with my rubber sword and cellophane X-ray glasses.
Who said my life was green Kool-Aid and goodnight kisses?
They didn't know my teeth were wiggling loose,
my chemistry set had poisoned the laundry,
my turtles were swimming up from the toilet bowl,
my mother was saving her temper for after the last photo.

Citizenship

For this merit badge, I reinflated my tires,
rode my Schwinn to Town Hall, chained
both wheels to the bench with the town seal:
General Putnam plunging his white horse
down Putnam Hill to escape the redcoat British.
I told the guard I needed to see the First Selectman.

For archery, I'd nailed five bulls-eyes in a row;
cooking, baked potatoes under coals;
hiking, climbed Rattlesnake Hill;
first aid, practiced tourniquets on a dummy;
survival, sparked birch bark tinder with rock and file;
knots, mastered the hangman's noose.

The First Selectman asked what I wanted to know.
He wasn't old, but was so bald I could count
each hair if I wanted to. His varnished desk
reflected his white shirt like spilled milk. I asked
why my father never finished his grapefruit
before rushing late to the train. Why my mother

toasted *The Galloping Gourmet* with her lipstick
stained wineglass, then heated us chicken pot pies.
Why my brother stayed home sick from school
to watch TV soaps in his bathrobe, growing claw
fingernails and stuffing popcorn down his pipe.
The First Selectman patted down the bump

in his tie-clipped tie and said, "When I was your age
I thought I had it made. Captain of the Webelos,
$4 a week caddying golf. Then certain things
made me realize my family was all I had.
You may not like them. But you'll learn love
isn't always easy. When it's hard is when it counts."

Riding home, I stopped at the creek rope swing,
stripped to undies. Who cared about citizenship?
I swung back and forth over lazy eddies,
swung so high that crows flew scared from trees.
My body tingled, as if trying to grow feathers.
Letting go, I grabbed at clouds before my great fall.

My Mother's Codfish

Her cork bulletin board's crumbly
with thumbtacks and photos, memories
she doesn't remember after strokes
confined her to a wheelchair. I Kleenex
smudges and dandruff off her glasses,
unpin the curled Kodak to hold before
her wandering eyes, tell her again
the rest of us caught nothing
but dogfish the charter boat captain
dehooked, bending their gray snouts
to crack loud necks behind gaping smiles.
He tossed their two-foot corpses in our wake,
toy models of deadly sharks below.

She sits in her lighthouse bathrobe,
my gift to remind her of Maine vacations,
but she thinks Maine is her diaper nurse now.
I tell her again she reeled in the champ.
The captain grabbed gills like duffel handles,
dumped the codfish on the deck with a thud.
It wore its hook without expression, button eyes
turning milky blind. We sponged water on its gills
to help the giant die in peace. On the dock scale
her catch hung taller than we boys stood,
squinting for the Kodak. Thirty years later,
I smile at our uniform blond bowl cuts,
but wonder about our grave faces.

I tell her again she had the best idea:
on our vacation diet of pizza and ice cream,
we had no use for such a fish, so we brought it
to Herman's in the village that handled everything:
fishing gear, groceries, baseball magazines, the mail.
The wooden floor smelled a hundred years old.
By folding the tail, Herman squeezed the codfish
into an old-time soda chest filled with picnic ice bags.
"She's a monster," he said. "But we got her all in."
His overalls, smeared with cod scales, sparkled
like a movie gown. "Shall we dance?" he asked,

gathering two boys in each arm, his beard ripe
with cherry tobacco. He spun us round the floor
and sang us whaling songs to calm our dizziness.
My mother knew them all from childhood.
I'd ask her to sing one now, but she slurps tea
through a straw. Her afternoon snack
brought by the nurse is what she's waited for.

Dog City

Only once, lost on our way to Jack-in-the-Box,
did we find the glass office tower, forever
unfinished in the ghetto neighborhood,
a campus rumor like lab monkeys on LSD.
But it was true; under naked light bulbs
a wolfhound paced the cement lobby floor
littered with dried turds and dry water bowls.
Spotting us, it trotted over, yellow-eyed,
and smeared its rubbery nose on tinted glass.
We tapped the pane. The dog snarled and raked
the window with its claws. We dared each other
to go in to touch the red letters graffitied
by the elevator, "Dog City."

Lerner insisted he would have, no sweat,
but he had a problem set to finish before bed.
Baxt had to call his girlfriend. Yaz's ankle sprain
hadn't healed from hallway Frisbee. Ralphster
urinated in the hedge. Oppie cracked, It's
The Church of the Damned. Always stoned,
everything reminded him of cheeso horror flicks.

I stood there longest, trying to conquer a fear
I didn't know I had: not the dog, but the elevator
leading to a room so terrible and important
the wolfhound guarded the lobby with killing glee.
If only I could get there, I'd never want to leave.

Passions of the Desert

At the last garage after Needles, the sun-
leathered mechanic in overalls, so drunk
he had trouble connecting his lighter
to his cigarette, fumbled jumper cables.
The claw he clamped on our Civic battery
fountained sparks over his palsied hands.
Not wanting to watch an electrocution,
we carried our Frisbee around back to
a desert runway with a solitary Cessna,
wings tied-down, propeller blades bungee-
strapped. The boy who watched us toss said
summer highs hit 120, but winds were worse.
Once the plane got loose and flew into a cactus.

Two days late to campus from geo field trip,
we'd learned: go easy on the tequila worm
and morning check sneakers for tarantulas.
We hauled a trunk load of discoveries,
pieces of the planet we'd chipped off for ourselves.

The mechanic said the alternator was dead,
took three bucks, told us to spend the rest
on a Buick or a Chevy. He turned his lighter up
until the wind wrapped flame around his face,
igniting half his cigarette at once. The boy said
the old man hadn't grown back eyebrows ever.
"Hotter than hell," the mechanic grumbled,
"but I own it," explaining why he'd stayed
years after I-40 ten miles north stole his traffic.
We wondered what we'd give eyebrows for,
what passion could be worth more than our face.

One Night in Kingman, Arizona

On the bungalow motel's cave like stucco ceiling
lizards ran loose. A black-and-white RCA made
this evening's train wreck look like vintage history.
But we'd seen it for ourselves beyond city limits:
freight cars toppled down track embankments,
still coupled on their sides. Belly smoke rose
to shroud the moon, a coal-faced monk pondering
the damage. Small fires burned beside the tracks,
as if gypsies camped to scavenge after daybreak.
Chickens soldiered through our low beams
toward desert blackness. Defying cruiser tops
spinning red, we stoked our hash bowl, knowing
we'd never see such sights again. We'd heard
radio preachers warn the sky itself would burn.
Nothing shown on TV later could tame this land.

The Prophet of Potrero Hill

-- San Francisco

Remember the gargoyle carved in a gate post
that shimmering afternoon our mushroom tea
tasted like woody soup? Its weathered frown
guarded a yellow Victorian atop Potrero Hill.
After our slow-motion thigh-burning climb,
we were amazed by this prophet on a fence
with splintered eyes and tiny tusks in its beard.
Remember what it said? "Kiss me, graduates,
so you may lead a long and surprising life."

You'd rented a floor-through with a Jacuzzi
and a gay landlord upstairs who greeted us
in new camel boots and ironed white T-shirt.
"Mi casa es su casa," he told you. "Whatever you need
—spices, laundry soap, condoms—just knock."
He jacked up the speaker volume and surprised me,
a middle-aged man lip-syncing Talking Heads,
"This ain't no party, this ain't no disco. . ."
For air guitar he swung his arm like a hammer.

"A producer," you whispered. "He sells Quaaludes
to Emerson, Lake & Palmer." He'd discounted you
a synthesizer to compose your first album. He told us
to hike up the hill. "The views are fantastic on shrooms."
Yet we stopped in the yard, enchanted by an old bathtub
half-sunk in weeds, half-filled as a sunflower planter.
"How psychedelic," we agreed. "How Frank Zappa."
We'd photograph it for your album cover, maybe
my novel. A philosophy major, I had serious plans.

Out on the curb we sat to admire the concrete army
of skyscrapers downtown. "What a view for an earthquake,"
you said. "We'd see San Francisco topple into the Bay,
like, from the front row." We vowed to meet here again,
no matter where our lives might take us, to watch
the catastrophe on mushroom tea. Twenty years later,
I've learned this city won't tumble so easily,
yet friendships vanish without a word.

The thigh-burning hill I climb this morning
still has Victorians, VWs, parked wheels
turned into curbs. But where is the gargoyle
with cracked eyes and sun-warmed wooden lips?
Remember what it promised? How silly,
kissing a gate post. How sad, not to do it again.

All That I Quit

The cowhide briefcase, the brass lock dialed 0-0-0
for my resume and scavenged *New York Post.*
The sidewalk vendor hawking bullwhips
and Malcolm X cassettes outside Grand Central.
The New Yorker address on 43rd I avoided,
walking 42nd and 44th detesting my cowardice,
until, finally, I boarded the old-fashioned elevator
with a folding metal gate and wondered if the derby man
with white hair in his ears was the horse track correspondent,
or an Irish poet, or Shawn himself. Silently I rehearsed:
"I'd like to apply to be a fact checker.
I'm looking for an entry-level position as a fact checker."
But he stepped off at an insurance floor.
The receptionist took my resume, phone cradled
on her shoulder. Going down, regretted what I'd listed:
Eagle Scout, Dormitory Monitor, Creative Writing Minor.

Waited for my father outside a Japanese place on Fifth,
plastic sushi in the window, red salmon faded to kidney.
A bum rattled his cup: "What are you waiting for?
Tell God you love him today." I unloaded all my pennies.
Squeezed into a booth, my father collar-tucked a napkin
over his tie and ordered chicken teriyaki and diet Coke.
I asked for chopsticks with my sushi deluxe
and Sapporo Draft. What could we discuss?
My mother's latest episode on sweet vermouth?
His morning forecasting interest rates?
Mine in a record shop browsing punk imports?
Finally, the waiter brought our check
under a quartered orange. My father asked
if I wouldn't like the name of the vice president
in charge of writing annual reports.
I told him, no thanks. Then he asked if I'd like
to meet by the information clock for the 5:17 express.
No, I said. I planned to catch the 3:48.

Nothing more to say, except we exited into a miracle.
There stood Muhammad Ali in a cashmere coat
squeezed into the bus lane by mobbing fans
waving papers like parade-day flags for his autograph.

Behind bodyguards the champ raised pudgy hands.
Ali, he scribbled, a scrap still in my wallet,
the only souvenir from a dismal time. I saw fame,
but when I turned my father had gone back to work.

The Night I Saw The Clash

Back from my first business trip, three weeks
studying paper mill chemistry in Appleton, Wisconsin,
where place mats read, "Twelve Steps to Making Cheese"
and the diner cowboy nursing coffee and a Camel
greeted me each morning: "Hey Manhattan!
Bet you've never seen a tornado." No,
but bored silly by my Best Western suite
I'd ridden the mechanical bull in a stripper bar.
Dancers wore striped thongs and pasty stars
adding up to flags. The waitress called me "Hon."

Back in Times Square, my suits dumped
at the cleaner's, a quarter gram in my pocket,
meeting my girlfriend for the new Wim Wenders,
when a teenage New Waver in pressed-cuff jeans
hawked me two tickets to The Clash at Bonds.
Christ! The Clash had owned my brain for months:
"London calling to the faraway towns.
Now war is declared. Battle come down.
London calling to the underworld.
Come out of the cupboard, you boys and girls."
Already I could hear the mighty bass goose-stomping
across stage, the singer belting out anarchy
under concert lights landing like UFOs.
Fuck Wim Wenders! I had to rescue
my girlfriend from the cinema now!
My life in paper chemistry was over.

I hustled up Broadway and nearly collided
with two street urchins chased by a lumbering wino,
baggy crotch piss-stained the size of a continent,
bandaged hand wagging a shiny knife.
His chimney soot hair and scabby red face
made him a drunken Devil to these boys,
who'd slashed his pants pockets for loose coins
and now ran for their lives, thrilled to cheat death.
But he smiled at me with gold in his teeth,
Odysseus disguised, the warrior who'd crossed
the mocking plains and returned to test citizens
to see beneath his filth. I vowed, My God,
don't ever let me leave this town again.

Love, Falling In

Punchbowl tipsy, we stepped onto the terrace for air.
You told me your medical history: two abortions,
six months starving on peaches, group therapy
with Ted Kennedy's ex-girlfriend and a lapsed Baptist
who cruised Grand Central bathrooms, embarrassed
by his toupee. But you were better now, and I was 23
at my first high-rise party, feeling the full height
of the 38th floor, pouring my drink over the railing
to stretch into a six-foot snake with glassy skin.

"Here's where that weird suicide jumped," you said.
"Wind blew him through a window downstairs.
Nobody knew, until they tracked blood drops
from the elevator and found him back up in bed."
"How ironic," I said. "To leap and miss."
"Totally bipolar," you said. "He married the next week."

At the punchbowl reloaded with tequila sunrise,
we dipped sticky cups and toasted the Fourth of July.
Fireworks blossomed over the apartment horizon,
day-glo dandelions in a sky too velvet for stars.
Your purple blouse strained buttons over a tan bra.
The gap in your front teeth meant something sensual
in Chaucer that I tried to recall from sophomore English.
Your shyness was inviting. You asked if I knew
The Merck Manual of Medical Information
spread like a library dictionary on its own lectern
by the stereo turntable. I didn't, but wondered
what it said under "Love, falling in."

Whitey's Last Stand

My parents had sandbagged my teenage bed
with *Commentarys* and *National Geographics*,
so for post-arrival sex I chose their king-sized
Posturepedic with its feather-leaking spread
forest green as a sleeping bag. My mother
believed eider down softest on her hip bursitis.
Every afternoon she napped to ease her pains.
Every night my father fell asleep in a TV chair.
Whatever happy accident produced me
came long before her craving for vermouth
hidden behind the Ajax on her cleaning shelf,
or my father's bitterness toward Democrats.
But they'd gone to Mount Desert until August,
so I'd snuck home for a weekend in Connecticut
to escape my Hoboken railroad flat, an oven
without AC. My girlfriend smelled of coconut
and salt from our day at the Greenwich beach.
She'd been so impressed with my WASPy roots,
a Brooklyn girl, herself, with Beatnik parents.
Now she delicately pulled a white needle
from the bedspread that fluffed into a feather
she used to tickle me down the spine,
while I flipped pillows to hide the cat hairs,
then knelt to lick her where it counted.

The awful scratching sound pulled me back.
Whitey, my old cat, climbed burlap wallpaper,
black hair nearly bald, body gray as dryer lint,
a gargoyle by the ceiling, his eyes blistered glass.
I'd saved him years ago, the runt with a crooked
saber tooth, a comma closing outside his mouth.
His perfect blackness, save for paws eraser pink,
made him my ally against suburban niceness,
where even the Doberman was called Polly.
Irony-addicted at fourteen, I named him Whitey,
tried training for a week, calling out the door,
"Here Whitey, Whitey, White-White-White, Din-ner!"
All he really learned: the can opener puncture sigh.
Never one to knead or cuddle, he'd held his own
against our lovable late collie, the garage skunk,

and Polly. Only at 3 a.m. would I wake to find him
napping by my feet, my surly prince of darkness.
Now this dying cat clung below the ceiling,
tugging his claws snagged in stringy burlap.

Up from bed, I cupped his toothpick chest,
gingerly unhooked his nails. Light as socks,
yet he twisted to razor swipe my inner wrist.
I threw him in the hall, bolted the bedroom door.
My girlfriend covered herself with the puffy spread:
"Why didn't your parents take the poor thing to a vet?"
What could I say? Twenty-three and headstrong,
I'd wanted sweet revenge, fucking in my parents' bed.
The phone rang, a neighbor reporting Jersey plates
in our drive, as if thieves had arrived.

Oscar Night

In an East Village walkup with naked-bulb halls
our hostess drops the oven door for heat,
serves pot roast on paper plates, purple juice
swirling dangerously close to the edges.
Her bruises come from cramped furniture,
she explains, not S&M as friends think.
A freelancer, pencil stubs behind both ears,
she tell us her next Russian mob expose
better pay for her tabby's inoculations.
Slipping him gristle, she adds, in human terms,
he's 110. "Poor guy. Never been laid."

I settle into the zebra-striped lazy chair,
my feet stupidly raised, and peel the wet label
off a Mexican beer. My wife wants me
to appreciate her astrology friends.
"They're very smart," she'd said on the stairs.
"About something very stupid," I'd replied.
Already, she's dipping a napkin in a water glass
to dab the purple juice stain on her blouse.
She's anxious tonight. She over-tipped the cabbie
$5 coming down. Now the rail-thin blonde
seated yoga-style at the piano-bench table
whispers into her ear. All I can catch:
"He rubbed a fig down my spine
that hatched me out of my skin."
My wife nods. Once we read Yeats in bed.
Now we never stay home.

I stare at the stalactite gray ceiling foam
meant to muffle the piano, cave décor
for an amusement park ride. To be honest,
I haven't watched Oscars since *Towering Inferno*
lost Best Picture, so why did I tag along?
Suddenly, the TV, which has been spastic with ads,
freezes for the first silver gown parading the red carpet,
glittering with scales ready to come off in my hands,
a mermaid revealed. "Don't get excited," my wife scolds,
accepting the sweet potatoes. "They're silicone."

Our hostess hands her *The Supermarket Sorceress*
and says that to jinx Tom Cruise, she's lined her cat box
with his *Vanity Fair* photos. Delighted, my wife
reads aloud: "Skin is our largest erotic organ.
Sprinkle cayenne pepper on his towels.
After a shower he'll be your lion."
The way she smiles you'd never know
we haven't touched since her father died.

Moving Into My Cabin
--The Catskills

Hung a Cherokee bear mask by the door.
Loaded the pencil holder with wild turkey feathers.
Gathered an armload of dead branches
for the kindling box. Picked asters and goldenrod
for the old pickling jar on the table.
Decorated the windowsill with birch bark
and bird nests, a littered shotgun shell
for a humorous touch. Swept mouse droppings
off the shelves. Shook dust from the fireplace rug.
Noticed again the smell of the cabin:
thirty-year-old logs varnished whiskey brown,
charred chimney stones, wool blankets
passed from owner to owner.

Brewed pine needle tea. Wiped owl pellets
from the porch bench. Transcribed in my journal
the song of the stream. Listened to the red-eyed vireo
owning his treetop till sunset. Lingered
over sauteed mushrooms and stew.
Studied moths on the windows,
dozens, hundreds, fluttering, crawling,
staring with eyes tinier than crumbs, yet gold,
gold as fire. Stepped outside to join moths
at the windows, my first friends.

The Lumberjack's Beard

On a boyhood camping trip to Maine, I admired
lumberjacks' beards: blond pelts, red fox tails,
gray hornets nests, wing-spread waxed mustaches.
These men smelled of chainsaws, bathed in trout streams.
But my father feared my precocious reading of Kerouac
on our endless station wagon drive from Connecticut.
"Count for yourself," he said, uneasy in their trailer camp.
"The one in a goatee has seven-and-a-half-fingers."
But what did my father know, a bank economist
forever rushing out the door with shaving cream moles
missed on his chin, late for his train, the 7:48?
I did not intend to grow up to be a commuter slave.

Alas, at seventeen, my wispy beard left me nicknamed
"Cobwebs." In mirrors I saw myself as a Dutch painter
befitted for silk stockings, pantaloons, and pointed shoes,
not a scary hippie who'd seen flying assholes in the stars.

Losing my virginity didn't help. Nor did hitchhiking
to the Florida Keys with a pony tail and neck bandanna,
nor did reading Ginsberg and Ferlinghetti, majoring
in philosophy in California, protesting Apartheid,
or skiing eight days across the High Sierras, then driving
54 hours coast-to-coast on truck-stop coffee and beef jerky.
Nor did marrying an older woman with Anarchists
in her genes, buying a leather jacket on the Bowery
to wear ten years straight to CBGB, the Mudd Club,
Maxwell's by the coffee factory. Nor did reading
Journey to the End of the Night, sharing coke lines
backstage with a dwarf, rehabbing railroad flats,
or turning 35. Divorcing didn't help, either.

Not even my log cabin with wood stove and bullet hole
in the cathedral window. The Cherokee bear mask
hung by the door has varnished cheeks smooth as mine.
Do I not have hair on my chest? My balls? Lately,
sprouting from my ears? Did my grandfather not preach
Baptist sermons with eyebrows raised like flames?

No, I'm not a Marxist, beat poet, or wild hermit
with manifesto facial hair. Fair-cheeked, I shower
with a razor and harvest itchy stubble. My drain collects
whiskers for a mouse's beard. I rub my chin and ask,
Didn't Geronimo have a face like mine?

Procrastination

Now buried in a chainlink cemetery,
my mother left bureau drawers littered
with unfinished lists: "Get tweezers
for facial hairs. Food and witch hazel.
Benomyl powder for plants before mildew.
Harvard—Yale Nov 21st." All she finished:
vermouth bottles hidden on her cleaning shelf.
This morning hemlocks dump pillows of snow
on my cabin roof, as I desperately search
computer files for the draft I meant to finish,
inspired by Lorca's lines:

"Oh, savage shameless North America!
Stretched out on the frontier of snow."

Instead, I type my mother's name in asterisks,
my AOL password. The modem line whistles,
hisses, becomes an Arctic wind funneling
through a nose cone abandoned on tundra,
or whatever "remote connection" means.
The sand dial cursor waits like a guillotine.
"Redialing. Redialing." Finally, e-mails:
"penis pump mortgages urgent petitions."
Only one worth opening, an ex-girlfriend
forwarding a *New Yorker* cartoon:
"I'm told write what you know,
but all I know are writing workshops."

Procrastination is my addiction, I admit it.
I crawl under my desk to unplug the modem line,
then rip the phone wire from log cabin beams
like a poison vine, popping thumb tacks
to the phone jack. From my stone mantelpiece
I pick two deer bones, lash them in a cross
with phone wire, cut green camping cord
to hang this fetish from a ceiling beam noose.
I need to see the death of my procrastination.
I need to believe what my mother said,
"Write what you want. I won't read a word."

September 13th, 2001

-- The Catskills

For two days, I'd seen too much beauty:
the phone pole's Virginia creeper vine
raised the first autumn scarlet, goldfinches
plucked cotton from dried thistles, yellow
birch leaves navigated ripples one-by-one
in the drought-low stream. The blue sky
had no planes for two days—the wild sky
of our ancestors I'd never see again.
Finally, the weather broke. At my cabin door
I heard thunder bully over mountains,
smelled the first fat drops wetting stones,
watched hemlocks shake with brutal gusts.
I unplugged my computer in case of lightning.

I stripped naked and stepped into the downpour,
cold and pelleting, to join the crying world.
How I longed to have seen it for myself:
the towers smoking like chimney fires,
refugees in business suits, the ash blizzard.
But the forest hadn't changed, only history.
Rain pummeled ferns and puddled black
by the wood pile. Dirt spattered my ankles.
Hemlock needles stitched my feet.
A solitary lamp beckoned on the table.

The Howler Monkey's Eyes

My crumpled Kleenex catches yellow tears;
the nurse's dropper dilates my eyes in office dusk.
What price have I paid for touring paradise?

Honeycreepers, cuckoos, macaws, I went to
bird them all, especially the resplendent quetzal,
which dropped a beak-warmed avocado pit by
my feet, a tipoff to look up. My mother dead,
I spent my inheritance searching for species
that never reached her feeder in Connecticut.
No matter how limited her life, binoculars waited
on her kitchen windowsill. She hoped to see
a parakeet amid the cardinals and the chickadees.
"Birds are innocence," she said. "They still live in Eden."
Yet, by trip's end, I couldn't read without palming
my right eye that saw caterpillar fur on print.
Had I tracked parrots with binoculars into the sun?
Gotten a mosquito bite with a blindness virus?
In my hammock, I no longer studied the bird guide
bookmarked by my ticket home. Afternoons,
howler monkeys greeted thunderstorms with throat-
ripping groans like the terrifying dawn of man.
Birds fell silent, as howlers tore up the sky.

In his tailored suit the bearded ophthalmologist
secures my chin in the examination frame.
His hands smell of Phisohex, my mother's favorite.
She gave her eyes to science, her anxieties to me.
"Don't blink," he commands. His disk of light
sees through my mirrors of love and mystery
into tiny caverns of retinal hairs. I mean to ask:
Have you looked into a howler monkey's eyes
to see beyond their beady stares of blackness?

On his rolling stool, he dictates my condition
into a pocket recorder. I pay by credit card,
step out into a parking lot brutal with sunshine
and molten chrome reflections. Dilated, I see
the light that drove angels from this world.

On Becoming a Novelist

After stopping by my ex-girlfriend's one final time
and faking politeness as she weeded cabinets of my junk,
including a green energy drink can I distinctly recalled
buying as a joke, though she implied by avoiding my eyes,
"I can't believe I lived with a jerk who fell for such a fad,"
I find myself at the library, wasting an hour, seeking solace
in Fiction, when I happen upon John Gardner's novels,
hefty as Dickens, brooding with cover illustrations:
Sunlight Dialogues' blister-red rural stoplight
under a black-and-white Van Gogh night,
or *October Light's* hawk-nosed farmer
peering through glasses with enough distrust
to compel any reader through 434 small-print pages.
Two decades ago in my college writing seminar,
John Gardner was our hero, the demanding author
of *On Becoming a Novelist* and *The Art of Fiction.*
We trusted every word, no matter how hard to follow.

Yet I haven't read him in years and I'm not alone;
his old bestsellers, weak-spined in crinkly cover plastic,
fall open to pages that smell like an attic. As if to say hello,
I turn to his photo, an author surprisingly young to me now,
blond locks combed past his collar, eyes pensive as a folk star's.
In his farmhouse study he lips a long-stemmed pipe and
stares past the camera. I'll soon be his age, 49,
when his motorcycle spilled on a country highway,
scattering student manuscripts into thistles.

In college I flirted one afternoon on the pebble roof
of my off-campus house with an Indian-braided
poetry major in suede vest and braless white tank top.
She said I looked like Jack Nicholson.
"No," I replied, "John Gardner," my hair long and blond,
my pipe and tobacco pouch tucked in my pocket.
"Who has the patience for fiction?" she teased,
then slipped a handful of pebbles down my khakis,
and wondered aloud what it would take to corrupt me.

That night lying before the fireplace, we pretended
to see orange castles hidden among coals
and told fairy tales about kings and queens,
which had nothing to do with kings and queens,

and everything to do with what I hadn't done before.
After my housemates went to bed, we kissed,
her mouth full of such tugging I slipped my hand
down her jeans to discover no panties, but
warmth in her hips beyond what I'd imagined.
Removing my paw, she said, "I'm not that kind of girl,
despite what you may think about poets." Yet,
soon enough, we slapped waves on my waterbed,
an act surprisingly easy and finished almost before starting.
Lying naked, I admired small miracles: acorn nipples,
a feather chest scar from heart surgery at age six,
she said. She couldn't exercise strenuously or do drugs,
but no doctor could stop her from fucking.

"So, what's in your novel?" she asked.
"You are," I said. "The Indian lass who coaxes
the dragon from his cave to give fire to her tribe."
"Don't be ridiculous," she said. "We're modern people."
"Not in my novel," I replied. "In my novel, horses can talk.
Women still fly. Babies remember the birth of the world."
John Gardner said it could be so.

In the morning, her boyfriend wheeled his motorcycle
into the carport, spooking me out of bed into my jeans.
"Don't worry," she whispered, "we're liberated."
Still, I felt awkward, stalling him at the door, a T.A.
I remembered for hammy recitings of Old English.
He hadn't shaved. His ponytail looked frayed.
His leather creaked with impatience. He stared down
from a Neanderthal brow and headlocked his black helmet
under his elbow. "Didn't I have you in Chaucer?" he asked.
"No," I lied, feeling guilty for Cliff-Noting his god.
The Indian-haired poet appeared in her jeans,
chastely kissed his sunburned lips and winked at me.
"John Gardner, here, says he'll write a novel about me:
Gone with the Harley." I laughed, surely too loudly
for such a bad joke, but I was new in the world.
Paired in black helmets, they straddled the loud engine
and left with a skid mark. Settling at my desk, I packed
my pipe with cherry tobacco. No longer a virgin,
I could write truth and call it fiction.

What Is It About Christmas?

That I choose *Please Kill Me* from eight unwrapped books
to waste the afternoon on the couch, blizzard trapped
at my girlfriend's, reading punk rock's oral history.
Jewish, she's welcomed my father and brother to celebrate
her first tree ornamented with lights and stained-glass harps
to honor her musical career. She's watered the tree daily,
adding pennies for minerals to firm needles.
The first time we made love under its balsam scent,
I tossed her black bra on the treetop for a star.
"Leave it," she dared. "Your family will love it."
Maybe I should have explained our traditions.

My father, immersed in a three-pound Churchill biography,
slumps in his chair, white haired, partly deaf, barely
nodding as he paws butter cookies from her plate.
Settled in khakis and reindeer sweater pilled with age,
he's content with history. He's knocked off fifty pages
since lunch, pausing to ask twice, as he'll ask again,
if we think he'll be safe driving home tomorrow on bald tires.
The orange juice he requested for blood pressure pills
sits unfinished and not on its coaster. Sometimes
I could throttle him, but keep reading instead.
Switching to a World War I doorstopper, he asks if
I knew Ho Chi Minh was a waiter at the Paris Peace
conference of 1919? He thinks I'll be interested, as a Lefty.
I don't really answer. In *Please Kill Me* I read,
"When I wasn't getting laid elsewhere,
I went to Max's Kansas City every night."

My brother stands at the front door in white gym socks,
watching snow pile to the rural mailbox. Earlier,
he'd ripped plastic off everyone's CDs with a private fury
I didn't need explained. Now he listens to Shostakovich
as if to boast he wouldn't slum with *Please Kill Me*.
He only wore sneakers for this visit, so I know
he won't offer to shovel. He claims to lift weights
with a personal trainer and drink diet shakes,
but I still see twenty pounds riding over his jeans,
his ass crack whenever he picks up gift wrap to recycle.

A man-child, he lives with my father and studies
year after year for his masters in international relations.
Perhaps he dreams of going somewhere. At breakfast,
he nagged my father not drink eggnog on his diet.
Now he refuses my girlfriend's butter cookies
with a curt, "Too fattening." She shoots me a look.

The only one missing is my late mother. In red lipstick
and plaid, she lavished tinsel on the tree, played Burl Ives,
and told us how important Christmas was to our family.
But deep into vermouth she unleashed her fury
when we three men with catatonic baritones
refused to join carolers bearing candles in our drive.
"No wonder everyone ignores us the rest of the year,"
she announced, then accused me, correctly, of being high.

After strokes disabled her rage, we brought Christmas dinner
in picnic baskets to her nursing home lounge, motel like
but festive with plastic garlands and paper snowflakes
cut out by children. My father carved her ham into nuggets.
I snuck peeks at *Readers' Digest* abridged books.
Mentally-crippled, she smelled something burning
no matter how often we reassured her the building
was concrete, the tablecloth flame-retardant.

Spending Christmas night at the house, I didn't join
my father & brother for TV, but lay upstairs
on my teenage bed with *Naked Lunch*,
started many times since eighth grade.
Who could resist the opening line? "I awoke
from The Sickness at the age of forty-five, calm
and sane, and in reasonably good health except for
a weakened liver and the look of borrowed flesh..."
Now William S. Burroughs joins me again, his blurb
on *Please Kill Me*: "This book tells it like it was."

Really? Stuck at home after college,
unemployed in double-breasted pinstripes
bought to be a Mafia don one Halloween,
now worn for job interviews, I killed time
between appointments in punk record shops,

thrilling to every ruined guitar chord
in Richard Hell's "Blank Generation."
I'd never been a failure before, so I figured:
do it right. On the Bowery I bought a leather jacket
for the clubs: CBGB to study cryptic graffiti
for famous names; the Kitchen to follow the crowd
down emergency stairs in fear my ears were bleeding
from the cranked-up drone; Irving Plaza, where at 4 a.m.,
Johnny Thunders walked on stage in white leather,
though I don't recall the green junkie skin his friends
remember so fondly in *Please Kill Me*. To be honest,
I was a club wallflower who never got close to
punk's sick glamour. I rode the train home alone.

My girlfriend whispers, "What's with your brother,
staring at the blizzard? Is he afraid to go out?
And you? Obsessively reading *Please Kill Me*?"
She'd played harp at CBGB in a Dada rock band:
the stage stank of beer, the bathroom stalls
didn't have doors so junkies wouldn't shoot up.
"This sucks," she says. "Let's go skiing." So we do.
Dressed in fleece, we strap on touring skis
and pole across the road to a cornfield.
We glide down rows of stalk stubbles,
snow whiskers at dusk, then follow deer tracks
to a field where corn stalks remain standing,
brown as grocery bags and wigged with snow.
In gray light the falling flakes are invisible,
until we open mittens to catch them melting.
"Here's my favorite winter smell," my girlfriend says,
holding her wet wool to my nose. I love it, too.

Meryl Streep Has Brought All Her Pigeons

Poems of Hoboken in the 1980s

The Buckskin Bikini

Bland brick, the Hoboken cinema had no marquee,
but new posters taped Fridays to glass doors:
Dr. Butcher MD, Zombiethon 3. All winter & spring
I ignored them, lonely & 23 in my railroad flat
with cockroaches humping my toothbrush &
a steam radiator cold until dark. Days I temped &
mailed out resumes. Nights I missed college girlfriends:
Jennie in the Peace Corps now planted trees in Zimbabwe,
Stacy still upstate scooped ice cream at Ithaca Igloos
while finishing her portfolio. A few calls, a few cards:
they wondered why I'd picked Hoboken of all places.
What could I say? Saturday nights, the Clam Broth House
kitchen under my window stank like dishwater broccoli.
I feared I was condemned to jerk off for eternity.

Not until July heat so brutal my rooftop tanning chair
sank cloven prints in tar did I pay $3 for cinema AC &
Cannibal Vacation. The poster's buckskin blonde
roped to a tree stood on autumn leaves suspiciously
New Hampshirish. Nor did I buy the tag line,
"The cameraman was later eaten alive."
Not in the New Hampshire I knew. Yet seated
among kids yakking Spanish & brown bagging
coconut sodas, I wondered if I could ever go back
to Camp Witherbee. At night, we'd canoed across stars
floating on black water to the girls' dock, where
we'd never known what to do. We hooted like owls,
tiptoed quiet as Indians, tumbled back into boats
at a twig snap, giddy with cowardice.

On screen a blonde swimmer rises out of the lake
onto the dock, water beads speeding down
into her buckskin breasts. Commanding blue eyes,
militant cheekbones: what more could I ask for?
She shivers & rubs goosebumps from the cold water
I remember, water so cold I felt reborn climbing out,
then dove back in twenty minutes later
to sheathe myself in bronzed lake water light,
fish world where our rules no longer applied.

But on screen the buckskin blonde notices
her towel missing from its dock chair.
She stares above us into theater darkness.
Her eyebrows peak in horror. But I know
what she dreads is her obligation to scream
for the next ninety minutes. To hell with these kids
stinking of plantain chips who paid to watch beauty suffer.
I march down the aisle & lift her chilly wet hand
off the sandpapery screen, helping her balance
her big step down to the carpet. She's smaller,
but smells clean as a lake. Shyer in person,
she looks at my neck more than my eyes,
but smiles with relief. A country girl, I realize,
she's never seen the Big Apple before.
Arm-in-arm we exit, ignoring poisonous glares.
The old ticket booth taker chewing a cold stogy
doesn't look up from his boxing magazine.

In sunshine we walk down First to Riverfront Drive,
her callused bare feet tough enough for hot asphalt
& glass pebbles. Her buckskin has rapidly dried.
She has a North Country tan, light but with strap lines.
I wonder if her camp has a song, but don't ask.
She's stopped in her tracks by the first panorama:
downtown's twin towers to midtown's gothic spires.
I point to the Empire State Building that King Kong
climbed with his blonde. My heroine smiles,
so much sexier than the ape's frail fantasy.
A boy skids to a stop on his bike for her autograph
on his bicep. He saw her last night. "You were bitchin',"
he says, then wheelies to catch up with friends.
"Bitchin' means great," I explain, knowing how alien
Hoboken must seem. She glances down but smiles.
Her pearl pink lips must come from Heaven.

At the abandoned pier we use for a beach
old fishermen cast lines between weathered pilings,
boys catch crabs in lunch box-size cages.
Young men drink Colt 45s from ice chests

& wolf whistle at girls in bouncy tube tops &
door knocker earrings. Boom boxes salsa & rap.
Shish-kebab smoke travels the breeze.
I lead her to the pier's end to watch tugboats push
frothy mustaches upriver. I can tell she's enchanted.
What actress hasn't dreamed of Times Square?
We notice, below us, tiny whirlpools playing
hide-&-seek among pilings. One day soon,
I promise her, I'll write for a sports magazine,
read screenplays for a producer, book bands
at Maxwell's, do something better than temping.

But she's not really listening. Puzzled, she stares
at a pretzel cart, never having seen pie-sized pretzels
before, nor people frosting them with mustard.
Far from her lake country dock, she has lots to learn
about city life. I promise her a tasty treat & lead us
to an Italian ice cart, where a grandmotherly peddler
shaves her ice block & fills two wax paper cups.
I select cherry syrup which floods the ice scoops
like giant lipsticks. My heroine's first bites stain
her tongue crimson. She licks around the edges
to catch drips. At last my love drought is over.
I tell my heroine we'll kiss on my rooftop past dusk,
then lie naked where only nighthawks will see us,
crazy birds flying in circles, chasing their own tails,
which nobody in Hoboken watches but dreamers like us.

In salty winds her bikini straps flap, her blonde hair
catches on her lips. A red tear from her wax cup
dribbles down to her breasts. "Thank you," she says.
"But I'm only made out of light."

On the Prowl

Boo Boo's downstairs sold Jell-O shots
behind neon palms in the window.
McBride's up the block had used bar light
& sideways stares from the rummies
nursing 30¢ drafts. Out on Washington
Helmer's drew the jocks shooting schnapps
under a Bavarian clock carved with
a stag antlered head bow tied with rifles.
At Maxwell's Monday Night tryouts
the guitarist threw his pick to the stage:
only four of us in the audience.
Where were the girls?

The elfin booted blonde with mile long legs
on a Schnackenberg's stool wiping fingers
between fries to turn pages in Bret Easton Ellis.
After her blue eyed glance knifed my psyche,
I lost an hour on my pair of 50¢ hamburgers.
Or the shag cut brunette in a punk-buttoned
leather jacket down to her fishnets
flipping through record bins at Pier Platters
in search of Darby Crash & the Germs.
She bragged to the clerk she'd once dated Verlaine
before he became a world class prick.
The way she said prick kept me awake for a night.

Or the angel in nylon blue sweats walking her bike
on Waterfront Drive with a white cat cockpitting
a handlebar basket. As the pet sniffed my fingertip,
I noticed its eyes: one orange, one green.
"Your cat," I told her, "has David Bowie's eyes."
"You'd better not mess with Major Tom,"
the angel replied, quoting my favorite radio hit.
How had she landed in Hoboken without wings?
Her cheekbones wore blue dust from the sky.
The wind lifted her blonde hair like a flag.
I knew, if I let her pass by, I'd never be
happy again. Her regal cat yawned.
My fingertip held a blood pearl,
a bite without pain. I asked for her name.
"Sorry," she said. "Major Tom thinks he's a lion."

Arson Done Right

Fresh from Maxwell's with guitars still ringing
in my ears & somebody's beer on my sleeve,
I saw it all from my corner: the fire contained
to the top floor of the welfare hotel like campfires
along cornices, so rehabbers could gut the interior
& refurbish the brick facade. Firemen on ladders
aimed water hose cannons into smashed windows,
flooding the night with the smell of drowned coals.

My first night in Hoboken, before I had a phone,
I'd gone into that hotel. It had black & white tiles
old as the Jazz Age, plus wooden pillars & panels
varnished with gloom. Behind the counter, the clerk,
fixing an alarm bell with a screwdriver, pointed me
to a wooden booth scratched with numbers & names,
messages like scars. The receiver smelled of cold fries.
Staples had rusted into the varnish. I counted thirty six
of them before my mother answered, drunk as I'd feared.

"Where are you?" she slurred. For nine months
after college I'd endured her binges: drunk
after the dog got killed, chasing a car; drunk
after neighbors complained dandelions
had spread from our yard to theirs; drunk
for no reason at all except to stagger upstairs
to accuse me of failing to find a good job,
"You won the Latin Prize at Greenwich Country Day!"
What could I say? Madison Avenue wasn't hiring
in Latin right now? I'd saved what I could: painting
garages, trimming tennis club hedges, delivering
architectural drawings for a friend's dad. On nights
she had the furies, I'd slipped out to Scottie House's
to smoke Mexican & practice juggling. He was a master,
tossing up lacrosse balls in fountains & cascades,
but I didn't care. I couldn't wait to move out.
My mother had given up recycling, library books,
the garden club, everything I'd once known about her.

"Hoboken," I told her, gripping the greasy receiver.
"Hoboken? Hoboken's a ghetto." She refused to accept
what I'd told her about finding my own place. I said,
"Hoboken's getting better. You should quit drinking."
She hung up, banging the cradle before getting a dial tone.

The hotel fire was dying. I should have gone home.
The beer pad in my pocket had a blonde's number.
But I felt sad. The phone had rung a moment later.
"Yvonne?" asked a black man's baritone. I'd said
I didn't know Yvonne or anyone else in this town.
"That's too bad," he'd said, "Yvonne's the one to know."
He'd made love sound so easy he'd share it with strangers.
I stared at canvas fire hoses sprawled in the gutter,
wondering how they could spray so many leaks
from their ring joints without losing pressure.

The Leak

Mr. Pelaez heaved his bad leg up the stairs,
clunky as a cement foot. I waited, bucket in hand,
an enamel pot from the Clam Broth House kitchen
that I'd left under the ceiling tiles sagging like tea-
stained pregnant bellies. For a month, the leak
had migrated out of my kitchen into the bathroom
to plink bull's-eye in the toilet. Now it was back.
Mr. Pelaez, in his dinner jacket & floral cravat
from his maitre d's podium, reached my landing
& accepted the bucket, swirling the black water
around & around as if to see what was cooking.
"Your leak is very hard to fix," he cautioned me.
"We'll spread more tar on the roof."

With a broom handle he poked the sagging tiles,
spilling plaster dust. At least I'd get new tiles—
I was on my third set since moving in. Satisfied,
Mr. Pelaez sat in a chair to rest his bad leg
& wipe his moist brow with his floral cravat.
He smelled of cologne. "I saw your girlfriend
on the street," he said. "Take her to Atlantic City.
Show her a good time." But my girlfriend had left,
this time for good. One morning, she'd found
two cockroaches humping on her toothbrush
& shouted, "How the fuck can you live this way?"
"What way?" I'd demanded from bed. Hadn't I poured
borax powder like cocaine lines under the stove
& laid roach traps in corners? Hadn't the newspaper
said that cockroaches can survive nuclear war?
She threw the toothbrush at me, "Stick it up your ass."
Another thing I hated: her reliance on cliches.

But when I woke at 3 a.m., I wondered why
I'd been exiled from love. My college girlfriends
had both married bankers. My mother quit calling
after I told her to sober up. Now I'd grown obsessed
with the blonde bassist in the Individuals I'd seen
twice at Maxwell's & endlessly on their album cover.

My life wasn't right. So I flipped on kitchen lights
to hunt roaches. I pressed their shellacked backs
like thumb tacks to see what colors spit out:
phlegm green, goo gray. I couldn't explain
the differences. I was a hunter like Hemingway,
not a scientist. At my window in BVDs,
I gazed across the restaurant's rear roof downstairs
into the new condos romantic with moonlight,
white fridges & stoves as perfect as Bogie & Bacall.
Before my time, that building had been struck by arson.
Fleeing his apartment, Mr. Pelaez had crippled his leg,
falling off the fire escape. Plus, he'd lost his wife.
Now he lived two flights below me.

"Don't worry so much!" He rose from the chair.
"Come downstairs. I've got a new piranha, a face
you wouldn't believe." I followed him down
to admire the magical kingdom in his fish tank:
purple nightclub lighting, candy colored pebbles,
a porcelain mermaid with tiny red stars for pasties.
I studied her sugar white face & suddenly knew
blonde hair & blank eyes could be mine again.
It was the goldfish tail floating like leftovers &
the toothy piranha with all the time in the world
that foretold a future I didn't want to believe.

Meryl Streep Has Brought All Her Pigeons

A few brown & white, the rest gray as smoke;
they could be Hoboken's own crowding my kitchen,
though cooing with hisses that sound Polish.
Gray cloaked, Meryl looks frail from her ordeal,
seated with starved fingers twigged in her lap.
Her green eyes appear clear, but blue veins worm
her bony forehead; her hood covers for baldness.
But I know better than to mention the camps.
She has arrived & I have the right teas.
Last month, I cured my mother's drinking.
Vermouth tastes worse than vinegar to her now.
I put on my kettle & consider what to give Meryl;
even her eyebrows are lost. Like a shepherdess,
a model of patience, she watches her flock
jostle & bob & prance on pink feet.
They must be famished from their long flight,
so I sprinkle corn flakes all over my floor.
Is American cereal too large for their beaks?
They toss up flakes like confetti they celebrate
but can't eat. Who would have guessed pigeons
need help? But we live in a strange world.
Step by step, I crush flakes into crumbs,
gathering birds behind me, a pecking parade.
I could lead them down to the street to show off
my famous visitors: Meryl Streep's pigeons.
"Is Hoboken safe?" she asks. Her worry line
cuts deep between eyebrows. Chicory tea
will cure that. "Definitely," I reassure her.
"I've never been mugged. Everybody knows
everybody. The neighborhood's friendly.
It's Frank Sinatra's hometown." I figure,
as celebrities they must be casual friends.
"Why are there shoes hanging from wires?"
She's staring out my window at sneakers &
cleats that kids tossed up after the season.
"Oh, that," I say, charmed by her curiosity.
"That's a local tradition." But Meryl frowns
& holds a raw knuckle to her lips. My mistake:
where she's from empty shoes mark the missing.

"I'm sorry," I say, only to be interrupted by
furious wing clapping. A damned Hoboken
pigeon has jumped down from the windowsill
to steal a corn flake. It's joined by six bullies,
chesty brutes forcing Meryl's birds to cower
from cereal the locals devour. "Get the Fuck out!"
I shout. But my kicking & arm shooing
don't frighten these thugs from the rooftops.
It's Meryl's flock that flies, funneling out
into blue sky, rising in the shape of a robe.
She's gone even before tasting her tea.
Every morning I wake with such loneliness.

Matchmaker

The old joke shop went all out for Halloween.
A straw witch rode the awning flagpole for a broom.
Plastic dog poop lay on the steps. The door opened
to a canned recording of breaking glass. My date said,
"You must love this place." A Wisconsin blonde,
she considered Hoboken tacky. Plus, she thought
she'd get away with magic markered whiskers
as a cat. But I knew Mrs. Kirschner waited,
celebrating the holiday in an orange blouse,
while resting her bad hips on a stool & reading
the *Jersey Journal* through bat wing glasses
down her meaty nose. For generations, she'd dressed
boys & girls in fantasies: angel tights with lacy wire wings,
ghost ponchos, & black Dracula capes also good
for Batman hung racked from ceiling pipes.
I donned Reagan's rubber mask & announced
with a chortle, "We begin bombing in five minutes."
"I don't think so," said Mrs. Kirschner, eyeing me
above her glasses. "Not if you want to impress a lady."
"Thank you," my date said. "Bonzo's bad enough on TV."
We'd met last week at Maxwell's during ½ Japanese.
She studied theater lighting in Manhattan & thought
Meryl Streep was the greatest. "What would you
like to be?" I asked. A plastic fanny mooned us
from under counter glass beside a $1 million bill
with a joker for President. "Why can't I be myself?"
she asked, a milk-fed blonde in jeans & leather jacket,
who only smoked at parties. "Not on Halloween,"
I insisted & crowned her with a witch's hat,
tallest in the shop. "I can't wear this," she protested.
"It's like a traffic cone." Mrs. Kirschner understood.
She gave my date a black party mask with a beak-sharp
nose. "This puts mystery in your eyes." So it did.
Shielded by black, her blue irises no longer
came from Wisconsin or anyplace I'd known.
For me, Mrs. Kirschner had a pair of devil's horns
& red face paint in a tube. "Forget about the maiden,"
she said. "Go for what you want." The rose she gave us
had silken petals & thorns dipped in poison.

The Red Dress

The day I hit bottom, fired from Speedos
for spilling my Coke into the copy machine,
I saw the red dress that invaded my brain,
a hip hugging mini with a porthole bare tummy,
a blonde lost in her Walkman on the PATH platform
still coming home from last night at the clubs.
In red ankle boots she strode past the cop
raising his pad over an olive skinned thug
on a bench & demanding, "What race are you?"
The thug wouldn't answer, but watched the blonde
skirt his puddle of blood on the platform as if
it was melted ice cream. I wanted to shout,
"How much blood must a man lose before
you take notice?" but instead followed her
to the fruit stand, where she sniffed buttons
on melons with a nose perfect as Hollywood.

She was everywhere: at Maxwell's side awning door
finishing a cigarette before stepping into the band's limo,
or upstairs with a white wine in the art gallery window
converted a month earlier from a boxing gym,
or seated on church steps during a movie filming inside,
rolling a cold beer on her temple while laughing
with a leather-panted, leather-faced old British glam.
She made me feel I knew nobody but my landlord.

Finally, at the bakery eating my afternoon cookie,
I spotted her alone on the sidewalk, glancing in at
the triple-tiered wedding cake with candy figurines
of Elvis & Marilyn united forever. I paid up &
followed, stalling at the pharmacy window,
until she came out with a toothbrush-sized bag,
& long legged it down Washington past winos &
baby carriages, lost in her Walkman, red ankle boots
eating up distance, red minidress flouncing without cares.
Here I was deep into the failure of another hot day &
she was still coming home home from last night
when at 3 a.m., shaken by dreams, I'd hunted
roaches by flashlight under the stove. Just once
I'd like to get into the VIP room at a club.

Lightly tossing her hair, she cut through traffic &
headed down Fifth, dodging an old timer with a cane
& a rolled-up *Jersey Journal* in hand. Were we headed
to the park across from the library, where, lately,
I'd wasted hours in Fiction? Maybe she'd browse with me.
Or sit on a bench & discuss Iggy Pop & the Stooges.
Or buy Popsicles at the cart pushed by the Cuban
in limousine tinted shades, who only charged children
a nickel. Suddenly, she unlatched an iron gate
& ducked under a brownstone's front staircase
to her cave-like basement door. Tired curtains
in barred windows didn't hide the puke
linoleum floor. How could she live here?
I grabbed the toothbrush-sized bag she dropped
on a garbage can lid to save her from littering.

What was my problem? No job. No sex. Nowhere
to go. The next afternoon I waited with flowers
two staircases down. I'd filled in once for a week
as the third man on a moving van, so I had ideas
for her new place: a garden studio on Bloomfield,
a converted loft on Clinton, if she didn't mind walking.
To celebrate, we'd dine at the Brass Rail upstairs,
the French place with waiters in vests & tux shirts.
I'd ask: What was her name? Where was she from?
Did she prefer lobster to steak? Pacino to Hoffman?
Did she wear her red dress in winter under a coat?

By nightfall, I sat in my puddle of loneliness,
hating the day I'd chosen Hoboken after college.
The red tulip bouquet had gone limp in my hands.
The cop car had come round the block three times.

In the morning I put on my coat & tie last worn
for graduation two years ago & took the PATH early
into Manhattan to join a temp agency. The first week
I typed library catalog cards into a computer,
the second I proofed medical journals.

In a month I had a regular job, assistant reporter
for *Metallurgy Week* & a boss who promised to train me
to be as good as the *Times*. After a year I was engaged
to Rebecca who worked for the Mayor's office
in community affairs. A curly haired spark plug,
she called me her mensch & loved sex before breakfast.
She called Hoboken my blue period. "You had to let go
of your mother," she said. Sundays, we rode bikes
from her Village apartment across the GWB
to the Palisades for picnics in civilized New Jersey.
I'd finally started a good life. But I never stopped looking.
Every time I saw a red dress I knew I could lose everything.

Marathon Training

Marathon Training

I passed ship propellers stacked two high,
boxing bags racked in a factory window,
the last of industrial Hoboken hanging on.
I smelled acrid air by the white chemical plant
where busy sprinklers cast water umbrellas
over flawless sidewalk grass, the only success
for blocks. Yet I preferred these back streets
below the Palisades: the brick pistol range
without windows, the paved lots cracked
with prairie weeds, the quiet without traffic.
Once Hoboken made 800 kinds of pencils,
birch beer, straw hats, & J.P. Morgan's yacht.
Now these forgotten blocks made my legs strong
as iron. But in the projects I saw young men
dangling Yoo-hoo bottles between seated knees.
They were so skinny, but I did all the running.
All those lost jobs were ghosts at my heels.

"Vezzetti! It rhymes with spaghetti!"
--Tom Vezzetti, Hoboken Mayor, 1985-1988

Our sidewalk mayor in his carny barker tie,
boater, & bullhorn he called the Liberty Bell
entertained—or at least cowed—two elderly ladies
on a bus bench with his complaint; his new shoes
too tight to walk to the cobbler, so he'd called
a police cruiser. Marathon training with iron thighs
& bottomless lungs filled with roasted coffee air
from Maxwell's factory, I tried to slip around
Hoboken's mayor, who grinned with bad teeth
from German pastries, his 60-year weakness.
He'd told the *Reporter* he couldn't afford dentures;
all his money down to the pennies fighting his recall.

"Who's the woman you're running from this time?"
bullhorned the mayor. Stopped dead in my tracks
in nylon shorts light as a handkerchief, I admitted

I'd gotten married last month. "She's crazy,"
he told half the block. "Tell her congratulations
& tell her to call me if you start acting up."
From his lapel he unpinned an old carnation
I tucked in my waist band. A year later
he collapsed on stage, dead of a heart attack,
Hoboken's martyr who tried to stop gentrification.
My wife had kept his carnation in our wedding book.

The King's Flying Castle

I dumped my Hefty bag at City Hall Laundry
the afternoon Ronald Reagan flew low overhead,
a helicopter formation I'd seen in *Apocalypse Now*.
I joined fat-legged widows, Cuban waiters, rockers
in Ray Bans, condo rehabbers in dust masks & chalk
powdered boots, the mayor hugging his bullhorn,
all trotting down Seventh to the Feast of St. Ann's,
where Reagan somehow slipped past us to appear later
on the 6 O'Clock News, lobbing softballs at wooden milk bottles.
All we saw leaving: two identical limos with Secret Service
riding like boat bumpers. In the rear tinted window
a metronome hand gave us his blessing, the king
returning to his flying castle. Sadly, we knew
the Gipper was preparing his landslide.

Sunday Afternoons the River Smelled like Engines

I slipped through the pier fence hidden
behind the green copper terminal where
commuter trains sat vacant on Sundays.
Temping all week, I had no other time
to plan out my novel, *Hoboken Rising*.
For inspiration, I brought my cache of $1
paperbacks from Hoboken Vintage Comics,
where someone had unloaded college staples:
Sartre, Celine, Brecht, *Gravity's Rainbow*,
classics I'd skipped, too busy majoring
in misery over girlfriends. Finally serious
about literature, I piled old dock ropes
into a chair & held pages firm against wind
that tossed gulls on wingtips dipped in black ink.
I read the first line but not for the first time:
"A screaming comes across the sky."
What was it about Pynchon's masterpiece?
All summer, I couldn't get past his octopus
with Pavlovian training. My attention drifted
to washed up buoys trapped in pier piling eddies,
then the green Fuji blimp nosing overhead,
a sky whale bound for Newark. I stood up
& waved like an airport runway jockey,
pretending to redirect the beast to Bayonne.
My wife asked why didn't I read fun books
instead. "Let's go together," I replied.
"I'll read Keats to your nipples."
But Sunday afternoons she volunteered
at the church shelter, baking lasagna for forty.
"Literature's no substitute for helping others,"
she told me. But she hadn't read what I'd write.
"Sunday afternoons the river smelled like engines,"
was my first line. The rest could be anything.

In the Time of the Gipper

Behind my study door, I stripped gummy black varnish
from my grandfather's desk, polished the coppery grain.
Where he'd typed sermons during the Depression,
I'd write *Hoboken Rising*. But what should my novel be?
The story of Mrs. Delgado's tenement on rent strike
because green molds grew alien fingers reaching in
to lift up the ceiling? That was my wife's suggestion
now that she volunteered at the Tenant's League. No,
I had my own idea, a Stephen King-on-the-waterfront
after Ronnie Ray-gun pushed-the-button sort of book.
My hero would drive his Chevy down from Passaic
to find nobody here, just pigeons in the train station &
Shop Rite bags snagged in trees. No more young women
in business suit dresses & puffy sneakers rising up from
the PATH to squeeze tomatoes at the vegetable stand.
No more pier kids crabbing with lunch box-like cages.
No more old timers in fedoras on the City Hall bench
arguing over Hoboken's best mozzarella: Pasquale's,
Delfino's, Fiori's, Tudino's, or Biancamano's.
After Ray-gun's mistake, the cockroaches
would prove they could survive nuclear war.

On my polished desk I set up my college Olivetti
with an ink-clotted "p," then opened the window,
as an ocean liner honked on the Hudson, leaving
for sea. For six months, I'd saved every spare dollar
from temping at Speedos, riding third man on a
moving van, or waiting my turn on a law firm
messengers' bench beside a semi-retarded man
with sardine sandwiches foil-wrapped in his pocket.
Temping was hell. But now I had a whole month!
& I was a fast typist. By dinner I had twelve pages,
my first chapter finished. My hero had searched
Hoboken uptown and down to find no one around.
"How can you write a novel without people?"
my wife asked over linguine with red clam sauce,
my takeout treat from the Clam Broth House
downstairs. She would have preferred I get a real job
& write my novel from 6 to 8 in the mornings

like her MFA friend. "Don't worry," I replied,
ravenously working through garlic bread, too.
"I'm just getting started." But the next morning
& next afternoon, I sat frozen by the blank page.
My hero had a lifetime supply of pasta & clam sauce
in the freezer downstairs, plus all the time in the world.
What I couldn't imagine was how he'd resurrect
the country I wanted to believe in.

Our Craziness

June

Bearing a free watermelon, my bride in her gown
returned from the vegetable stand with the Korean's
wedding day blessing. The wino homesteading
our steps helped her unlock the rattly doorknob
& accepted a carnation he wore in his lapel
& sniffed for a week. For once, our cats didn't jump
on her dress, but sat with question mark tails,
as she opened a tuna fish can, their wedding day treat.
Even they knew we'd done something crazy.
Our license from the judge's chamber lay
on the counter. Before calling anyone, I lifted
her white lace to kiss the growing tummy I adored.

September

All those wedding gifts lost to the cats' antics:
champagne flutes, a silk scarf from Hermes.
Be reassured: we didn't marry for material gain.
But the finale? Nancy wiped her butt on the rug,
while Sid leaped from a radiator onto the fridge,
where for safe keeping we kept the salad bowl,
hand-blown in Vermont. Solid as glass brick,
but Sid nosed it over the edge onto the radiator:
fifty glass nuggets. Sid & Nancy: why did we name
our cats after a Sex Pistols thug & his groupie?
Because, after the miscarriage, they gave us the gift
every night of kneading our heartache into putty.

June

She opened *365 Chicken Recipes* to discover
a $100 bill she'd hidden years ago, a neurotic period
we didn't discuss. We celebrated at the Brass Rail,
reservations upstairs: linen napkins folded like doves
& crystal vase roses. Our waiter kept reappearing
to scrape bread crumbs, as if we were careless.
Her pate arrived to smell like my sneakers.

My coq au vin turned out to be chicken.
She admitted a bad day writing copy,
stuck first on explaining garage door openers,
then on directions for tub washing venetian blinds.
I said nothing about not writing my novel.
For dessert we shared Napoleon & Crème Brulee.

Too early for home we strolled to the cannon
on the tech college hill for the harbor view
of lower Manhattan's tuning fork towers.
Tugs shoved through wrinkled black water.
Trees shook salsa up from Waterfront Drive.
She said the City looked like a choir of angels.
She said she forgave us the miscarriage.
I said we were still young & lifted the necklace
of the George Washington Bridge from the skyline
to lay on her breastbone, our miracle now a year old.

I Feed Her My Heart
She Never Stops Eating

Poems Inspired by
Night of the Living Dead

Why I ♥ Zombies

They've let go of their pride.
They're not vampire aristocrats
spoiled by virginal necks,
or mummies older than Christ.
They're retired plumbers
in boxer shorts pulled snug
on beer-and-potato-chip bellies,
or housewives in dumpy nightgowns
wandering barefoot on the lawn,
hypnotized by crickets.
They're not Frankenstein's
monster with bolts in his neck,
or alien coneheads with 500 IQs
& rotten claw teeth.
They're volunteer firemen
with charcoal puffy eyes
from watching Carson night after night,
or secretaries softening faces
with cold cream before bed.
They're not bikers, hippies, or rednecks,
the stock villains of 1968,
but young men with good haircuts
& worthwhile careers,
teaching high school biology,
or managing a Chevrolet showroom.
All good citizens, they're eager to help
a young crew from Pittsburgh
film a low-budget nightmare
at an old farmhouse. Amid spotlights
slashing the lawn, they shuffle & groan
as cameramen kneel for closeups:
gunshots to the chest, spikes to the head.
They're thrown out & burned
like junk furniture. They have no idea
one day they'll be famous,
terrifying us by being so ordinary.

The Zombie Gene

I see it in the way my brother drives 45
on the highway, a company messenger
despite his master's degree. Entering rooms,
he no longer turns on the lights, just sits
in the dusk furrowing his brow. The winter
our mother died he walked at the beach
& pronounced himself cured. I wish

I could drive a tire iron through his forehead,
puncture his lethargy, release his ambition.
Instead, he still lives with Dad & nags him
over TV dinners to take blood pressure pills.
Late night in the den where we first watched
Night of the Living Dead, they now revere
Charlie Rose interviews. They don't understand;

in their back yard, deafening crickets mask
the slobbering chewing of a zombie
still wearing her old tennis dress for gardening.
I feed her my heart she never stops eating.

Picnic

Nobody cares if it's past midnight.
Everybody stumbles around the lawn
as if practicing their own special injury:
crooked feet, slack shoulders, lopsided jaws.
Upstairs, Mom sleeps off her night of vermouth,
while Dad left hours ago for milk. On TV
zombies picnic on barbecued forearms
& pale intestines like sausage links.
My brother unscrews Oreos for the cream.
He can't live an hour without snacking.
Last night after *Dracula* we threw eggs
at the witch's garage, but he missed
into the spruce. Dyslexic, he gets Ds in gym
for tripping. Diseases are his thing.
Last Halloween he went as leprosy,
or was it elephantiasis? Tonight
I'll teach him some courage.

I dare him to stand in the yard butt naked.
To my surprise, he marches out boldly
through dewy grass & the sawing of crickets.
He drops his shorts, puddled at his feet.
His stretch waistband leaves pink treads
on his pudgy belly. His willy's shrunken up
like a walnut, but so's mine from the chilliness.
The moonlight makes cave skin of our tans.
What's your special injury? I ask.
What's yours? He never goes first.
I've got a crush on Carol Shaw, I say by mistake,
but it's true; all afternoon at the beach
I couldn't stop staring at the butterfly knots on her bikini.
What's yours? I ask. *Don't have one,* he snaps.
That's cheating. Good reason to go back in
without being chicken. On TV the picnic is over.
The hero punches the coward one, two, three times
into an easy chair. *I ought to drag you out &*
feed you to those things! he shouts, a taunt
I repeat for the rest of the summer, no matter
how often my mother tells me to lay off.
There's nothing funny about dyslexia, she says.

My brother stood naked past the end of the movie
to prove something major out on the lawn.
What, I don't know. Thirty years later,
he still lives in our childhood house, a virgin.

The Good Father

But a wife drunk on vermouth he avoided for the night
by buying milk at a 24-hour gas mart up the Thruway.
In the morning she didn't remember all the ugly things
she'd said, but found milk in the fridge already opened
by their two boys for cereal & the cat bowl. By then,
he'd rushed off to the train station after coffee & grapefruit,
his doctor's diet to lose thirty pounds. Alone on the platform
as the 7:48 shrank down the tracks, he licked his thumb
& rubbed an old tie stain until the 8:02.

Then a Division VP, red-faced in his doorway, furious
his monthly figures were late. He promised to finish
by lunchtime & did, not even stopping to pee,
tabulating each column twice on his adding machine
that unspooled paper intestines on the carpet.
Trying to be tidy, he rerolled & bound the paper
with a rubber band from his wrist. At night his wife
asked why he wore rubber bands to bed; did he love her
less than his work? If only she didn't depend on vermouth,
he knew she'd trust him again. The Division VP had left
early for the Princeton Club, so he placed his figures
front & center on the man's chair.

At his favorite lunch counter on Lex for chef's salad,
he dipped a napkin in his water glass to work on
the tie stain while reading the *Post*. How stupid
could the Democrats get, picking Eagleton,
who'd been to a shrink? Nixon had nothing to fear.
But the movie page had a photo of a blister-faced man
in underwear chewing an arm like a ham bone;
how disgusting monster movies had gotten!
He decided once & for all; no more staying up
past midnight for his two boys watching such trash,
not with one son two years behind in reading,
the other a bully. No more zombie games, either,
stumbling stiff-legged to the dinner table,
then gasping as if choking on gristle,
upsetting their mother. His sons
should be learning their presidents,
not wallowing in defeatism and gore.

Whatever happened to the family that smiled
at each other over breakfast with milk mustaches?
The waiter served a salad ruined by dressing
the color of flesh. The good father refused,
then with no time to reorder ate his first bite.

The Silent Majority

At dinner all my father discussed was politics:
Nixon, Lindsay, Nixon, Weicker, Nixon.
Never the Yankees. Never his day at the bank.
Definitely not the Page Six photos of hot pants
I'd seen in the *Post* he carried home from the train.
No, his face turned red, scolding me to appreciate:
Nixon was an honorable man. He'd worked hard
to overcome poverty, awkwardness, the snubs
of the lucky & suave. Sure, the President
had made mistakes. Wage & price controls
were bad economics, Watergate a festering boil
that should have been lanced before press jackals
ripped into his flesh. But Nixon had fortitude.
He understood our dangerous world. Study his book
—& my father could name all six of Nixon's *Six Crises*—
learn how character is forged: does a man risk all
when all is at stake? Or does he back down?
My father pounded the golden spike of his argument,
his forefinger up & down on the table.

At fourteen, I knew what he meant: no pot in the house,
Cs grounded me for a month. The *Easy Rider* poster
of Peter Fonda flipping the bird had better come down.
Frisbees were for druggies. So were hacky sacks.
Be a tackling dummy, my father admonished;
you're still on the team like Nixon was at fourteen.

For Halloween I wore Nixon's mask: penis-sloped nose
& lumpy ball jowls. "Let me guess," I told neighbors
who stood mute in their doors before my X-rated face.
"You're dressed up as the silent majority."
Through the President's eyes, I stared at Americans
forking out candy & UNICEF dimes. Behind me
zombies waited for a taste of their brains.

In College I Found My True Calling

Freshman year, starved with munchies,
we snuck through maintenance tunnels
linking dorms to the students' Tea House
open till 11 for potheads like ourselves.
Over steamy dumplings we decided
Dingwell down the hall was a genius,
doing triple bong hits before acing
engineering take-homes. But Ryan
was a nerd & Bask was disgusting,
leaving crumpled tissues round his bed.
The girls in our dorm were C+ to B-,
except for Margo Riley, *Gent's*
Ms. Nude Volleyball though she'd deny it.
To see her white shorts on a bike
was to know why California existed.
But the problem was my mid-term paper,
comparing & contrasting Richard Nixon
with a zombie, that still sat on my desk
hours from being finished. It was obvious
from the way he smiled at hostile questions
& wore black wing-tips on the beach,
but I needed 2,500 more words. Meatballs
inside dumplings had distinctive faces;
I bit my father from crown to chin
for persuading me to take poli sci.

At 11 the Tea House kicked us out for quiet.
My roommate knew a piano room left unlocked
where he'd improvise for hours like Keith Jarrett.
I lingered in the maintenance tunnel to ring the bells,
five propane tanks clustered upright like torpedoes.
Wobbling one as a clapper, I made music so ethereal
it rose by steam pipes into dorms, a metallic calling
students heard from the radiators. All the worms
in their lovesick hearts were driven out by my song.

A Daughter of Zombies

Let's start with the bark-faced woman
hugging the matching bark of a tree
to devour a beetle with an appetite
verging on lechery: did her daughter
grow up to be a serial killer, cannibal,
pet torturer, guest sicko on Springer,
at least? Or did she become ordinary?
A manicurist, bank teller, or better,
a hospital nurse in rural Pennsylvania
where you'd think nothing ever goes wrong,
but does—with chain saws, ladders, deer rifles,
&, of course, alcohol, men, & vehicles. Sure,
she's seen miracles—fingers sewn on,
hearts shocked back to beating—
but never the dead reawakening,
not like her mother in bark makeup.
No, the dead simply looked a size or two
smaller after losing all prospect of moving.
After work she volunteers at the church pantry,
visits old family friends in nursing homes,
sticks to Weight Watchers, & keeps all regrets
about not marrying to herself. For videos,
she prefers romantic comedies & anything
with Steve Martin, but every so often rents
Night of the Living Dead to watch her mother.
Yes, her mother, the school librarian, who insisted
on Sunday dinner with linen napkins & grace,
plunges to her knees to savor that beetle.
Her bark face twists beyond pain
into ecstasy. What did the director say
to give her mother such freedom?

The Bachelor

He's the dead ringer for a graying James Dean,
his funeral suit poorly fitted to his lurching frame.
First seen in the cemetery, he wrestles a bratty
young hipster, who treats him as a joke, until he
thumps the pretty boy's head dead on gravestone.
Then he rises to lumber after the terrified blonde
in trench coat & heels that trip her in overgrown grass.
Hair askew, mouth agape, she looks back in horror.
Does she think he'd be so crass as to kiss her?
Be less than a gentleman when he ate her?

Even the music hates him like a Fifties alien invader.
Yet he sold Allstate insurance, served twice as
Rotary Club president, returned every call before five,
shaved even on Sundays before teaching Children's Bible.
At Christmas he chaired the Orphan Fund drive.
It was no secret he'd never recovered from Suzanne,
the spelling bee queen & cheerleader captain
who'd eloped with his cousin, the wise-ass mechanic,
who gave her six kids & a trailer yard of jalopies.
Her laughter soured like a crow's, while
the bachelor's good looks matured like a movie star's
no one could touch, not the McGillicuddy sisters,
Norma Rayburn, or the bank president's young widow.
At his funeral everyone hoped a secret paramour
would step forward, but none did. All he left,
his nieces & nephews said, was his generosity:
college savings funds for each of them.

Out of a brier swamp he stumbles after the blonde's
promise. He knows he wasted his life on a broken heart,
but now smitten again he's willing to risk everything.
With every step toward the farmhouse he nearly topples
over his crooked knees. He fights through a laundry line,
yet reaches the porch too late. She's locked the door.
His star turn is over. For the rest of the movie,
he's one of the crowd distinguished only by
the terrible rip in his funeral suit shoulder.
When zombies break in the door, she gives herself
to the bratty young hipster, her brother.

How Could You?

Oh, please! It was only a ham bone smothered
in chocolate sauce & only one bite. Plus,
the hand on the end was clay. Only in lousy
black & white could it possibly look like an arm.
I mean, goodness! Me, the Bake Sale Queen
as a flesh-eating ghoul? The gals all had a laugh.
But my Kathy, she had to find something.
Just twelve: don't ask how she saw the movie.
I'd hate to think her father took her for revenge.
Now she's taped a poster of a crucified monkey
to her door & I'm sorry, but *crucified* is the word.
She's gone holy against meat, accusing me
of vulture's breath. She eats nothing but greens.
When I worry her beautiful red hair is losing
its protein, she scowls, our colons didn't evolve
to excavate meat. Did I know, she demands,
our toothpaste was tested on rabbits' eyes?
I scream, do you want to give up your teeth?

Didn't she see my face made up like a moon crater,
my hair teased out in a tumbleweed?
It wasn't me. It wasn't me. It was all of us,
Betty McGuire eating a beetle from a tree trunk,
even our minister grabbing that poor girl by the neck.
We were just helping young filmmakers from Pittsburgh
be silly: chocolate sauce dripping down the staircase
for blood, painted Ping-Pong balls for a skull's eyes.
The poor blonde in a wig shrieking & shrieking
until she got it right. Believe me, nobody lost
their appetite for sandwiches at midnight.

Now I'm locked out with the crucified monkey.
At her door I hear canned laughter inside on the TV.
Jealousy? Was that why he took Kathy to the movie?
All his buddies got to be zombies: the Ricci brothers,
Bill & Randy & Slim from Happy Hour at the Cavern,
my brother, president of the Rotary he'd dreamed of
joining. But I wouldn't allow it. Not after his little fling,
his little *fuck-you* bottle of Parisian perfume I found

in his tackle box. Never again is that cheat setting foot
in this family house. His arm tasted so good
the audience squirmed when I smiled,
no longer starving for love.

The Nude Model with a Mortuary Tag on Her Wrist

How far did you walk from your cold table on wheels,
Smythe, Carol 40916? How many pasture fences
did you cross without scratches, road puddles
without muddying toes? Arriving late at the lawn party,
you mingle among wives in sack dresses
who envy your marble-white poses.
All the good husbands ignore how moonlight
sculpts your buttocks & casts a tail down your spine.
The forlorn painter who loved you without a word
shuffles under a spruce, his cheeks peeling
like papier mache. He never mastered the flesh
you modeled with such ease. For hours,
you were his Venus, until you asked,
so politely, if you might pee.

Is it tragic you died so young?
Or do we prefer you this way?
Breasts firm as refrigerated dough,
dew-polished shins smelling of hay.

All we know: you left before the party
spilled into the house, nor in the morning
did the posse, sweeping fields, drop you
with a marksman's shot. Are you still walking,
luring farm boys down from their silos
to consummate in hay? Are you releasing doves
from their rib cages, leading you home to the sea?

The Ricci Brothers

Rudie & Richie, still so handsome
after driving drunk through the railing,
shambling in late to the party with killer
black lashes & cavernous eyes, bruised lips,
half-buttoned shirts & cologne like formaldehyde.
The women adore you, yet sense a great change:
no more necking in doorways, or trophy bras
slung over doorknobs. Not even the nude model
with marble-white skin catches your eyes.
What happened? No swigging back pocket pints.
No fire in your breath. No lust in your hands.
You wait patiently in line with zombies
to scavenge from the farm truck's burnt cab,
then kneel with hunger you didn't know you had
to grab squirmy intestines spilled on the grass.
The long tube you chew towards the middle
brings you to a last bite shared like kiss.
Rudie & Richie, in love at last.

Heavenly Father

I've honored your son, who tasted like all sons.
He recoiled at my appetite, whimpering,
clutching his spilled organs, suddenly unsure
suffering should be his way to holiness.
You will forgive him. You always do.
Like a moth he fluttered up from his flesh
toward a spotlight already preparing
the next scene. I was an extra till morning,
when I worked as a cashier. Heavenly Father,
his blood tasted like chocolate. Is that such a sin?

Child Star

Bitten by a zombie, the nine year old girl lay
feverish under blankets. Only one line
to remember & she didn't forget: *I hurt.*
Pale & solitary, she never fidgeted or needed to pee.
On a basement table she lay at peace
with her parents' bickering. Her bull-headed father
triumphed down the stairs to throw
his crushed cigarette pack & announce,
We'll see when they come begging me.
Her dark-haired mother with beauty-queen lips
sneered, *We may not enjoy living together,*
but dying together isn't going to solve anything.
Long bathed in strife, the girl ignored them,
yet noticed all the adults working on set smoked,
& a year later started herself: Luckys, then Parliaments.

She didn't think much of her performance, but
who can forget her? She rose at the end
in her Sunday dress to two-hand a trowel
over her head, revealing the slip at her knees,
then dug deep into her mother's chest to find
the love that she wanted. In black & white
blood splattered the walls as if she'd struck oil.

What Kind of Parents?

For 40 cents, Roger Ebert joined matinee children
escaping winter slush to sprint down the aisles &
hurdle into seats. Popcorn flew, golden meteors
in the projector beam. Ushers scolded with flashlights.
A pigtailed girl mitten-slapped her brother for farting.
Ebert covered his smile with his notebook. He fondly
remembered his own afternoons enraptured by monsters
half-reptile, half-ape, or the unforgettable 50-foot woman
he'd repeatedly married in dreams into his twenties.
On screen, a quarreling couple pulled into a cemetery
with funeral dark spruce & flash-bulb lightning.
As a knock-kneed ghoul stumbled into focus,
the children screamed to pin God to the ceiling,
safe again in their fears, their matinee glories.

Yet this movie grew boring. The house-trapped
survivors began squabbling & boarding up windows
& squabbling some more. Impatient with adults
acting like adults, the children migrated up aisles
for pee breaks & the snack stand: Juicy Fruits, Goobers,
Raisinets. The candied darkness let children enjoy
being children, Ebert decided. Their fantasies cost
a few cavities; but the world got saved week after week.
Yet these kids returned to scenes of zombies
spilling intestines like snakes in the grass,
chewing meat off bones but leaving the hands.
Silence smothered the crowd. No more fidgeting.
The mitten girl cried, cheeks shiny with movie light.
On screen the girl under blankets rose up as a zombie
& raised a trowel over her mother who pleaded *No!*
But the black-eyed daughter stabbed *Yes, Yes, Yes,*
digging out black blood gobs like pudding.
What kind of parents, wrote Ebert in the *Sun Times,*
dumped kids at a movie about flesh-eating ghouls?

My parents. Your parents. Parents everywhere
grateful for 40-cent babysitting, an afternoon free
to catch up on laundry, perhaps enjoy a couch quickie.

After the final burning of bodies, we filed up aisles,
chocolate spots & tears dried on our cheeks, &
waited under the marquee for our parents.
They didn't punish us for packing snowballs
with stone pits to batter parking signs.
They let us recover our courage.

Respect

To reach through boarded-up window slots
into the scared light of men with hammer & rifle.

To want nothing more than to touch human warmth
even as they sever your fingers.

To grab hold of the barrel as the bond between you
& pull with all the love you can muster.

To accept the shot to your chest,
the stain blossoming on your white shirt.

To bow with respect.
To raise your head slowly in shadows

that make caves of your eyes.
To let darkness stanch your wounds.

To step forward softly not to disturb worms.
To approach the window accepting

the sad truth: their terrible fear is the burden
that allows grace. To say nothing

no matter how brutal the shooting,
how many fingers you leave on the floor.

To lie on the lawn after the third shot
opens your third eye. To stare at the stars

which have seen this before & will see it again.

The Screenwriter's Cameo

At 4 a.m. he sidles in the mud room door,
tattered sleeve hanging from his uplifted arm.
The spotlight casts a corona on her blonde hair,
his heroine in an easy chair, far more angelic
than he'd dared put into words. Under hot lights
her perfume smells of roses. He acts his best,
despite his gimpy leg dragging a fold in the rug,
his left hand clutching his waist as if stabbing pains
are trying to reel him back out the door by a fish hook.
He has so much to confess, if only she'd notice.
He wrote his dreams into her role. Not just
the blonde hair, but her loyalty & church-going,
the way she stopped to listen to a music box.
He's not the lurid hack she might think.
Half the stories about bar girls & trailer parks
aren't even true. He'd introduce himself properly,
but his dry throat rasps, strip-mined by cigarettes &
laryngitis. He's worked so hard on this movie:
two titles rejected, drastic rewrites on set,
his old steel-town buddies recruited for extras.
Earlier tonight he made crew sandwiches for twenty.
No task too small: a pickle & potato chips on every plate.
Asking for a cameo after the professionals left for bed,
he thought he'd only wanted a minute of fame,
but now lurches forward so desperate & lovesick
he frightens himself with his talent for ruin.

He knows his bad Dracula makeup drips black
lipstick down his chin. He knows—he wrote
this movie—she'll only glance once, then run out
on his pathetic entreaties. The hero will tackle him
to the rug, hammer a tire iron into his melon soft head.
Yet his good hand reaches from his tattered sleeve,
as if he can touch the woman who wants him
to write from his heart instead of his greed.

The Final Survivor

Past dawn, the black actor crouches safely
behind the basement door thick as a dungeon's.
Unlike Hollywood's Poitier he hasn't said a word
about race, or smoldered & seethed, or sought grace.
All he's done was burst out of glaring parked headlights
into the farmhouse of his first movie to take charge:
boarding up windows & doors, finding slippers
for the blonde's chilly feet, organizing the escape
that failed when the farm truck exploded, caught by
burning gasoline spilled like a rope on the grass.
To make it back to the house, he'd torch-lit zombies
like scarecrows who'd tried to brush flames off their chests.

He rubs his face for the hundredth time to stay awake.
He's smoked his last cigarette. He worries
his mother will forget he's working all night &
won't return to her Pittsburgh apartment.
Sometimes at breakfast he recites Shakespeare.
She listens intently before coffee or putting on glasses.
A schoolteacher, she taught him literature counts.
Between takes, he's read serious books. No small talk.
He understands why Beckett restored silence
to a world without God. He has theatrical ambitions;
the Negro Ensemble Company has called
from New York. But, first, he's helping friends
finish this film. He taught the amateur cast
how to throw good movie punches. He nailed
his monologue with the rawness of Brando.
He played Mr. Cool to the hotheaded coward.
No silly Afro, ghetto shoes, or jive lingo;
he's acted with dignity; he's the final survivor.
His only regret, crouched safely at the door:
his white sweater smells ruined by smoke.
His mother will ask what she knitted it for.

At the first sounds of rescue—dog barks, sirens,
a robin greeting the day—he unbars the door
& steps to the window. He's living on hope,
enough hope not to know no one gets out alive.
The audience watches the white hunter take aim.

Searching for Willard

Remember the towns with emergency shelters listed
in round-the-clock broadcasts about flesh-eating ghouls?
Mercer, Sharon, Butler, New Castle, Beaver Falls.
Fresh out of prep school, I drove a campaign van
through *Night of the Living Dead* countryside,
trolling for votes with roof bullhorns for speeches
& brass marching music. If nobody showed,
I mooed at the cows, causing pasture stampedes.

Remember the opening scene of the Plymouth
swaying around curves into the graveyard
with puritanical spruces & cheap lightning effects?
I'd swear we got lost there between a Rotary Lunch
in Evans City & an afternoon call-in in Mercer.
The dotted shortcuts on maps ended too often
in gravel pits, junkyards, trailer parks, cemeteries.
The candidate deadpanned, *My favorite supporters.*

Where was Willard? That town seventeen miles
to safety for strangers trapped in a farmhouse;
they'd plowed their jalopy through zombies
till the gas tank exploded. Hadn't the broadcasts
promised them Willard had a secure gym &
the National Guard? They would have survived,
a happy ending for *Night of the Living Dead.*

Riding shotgun, Savini laughed at my search.
Forget the movie. Willard's not on the maps.
He told me again of Vietnam, where horrors
weren't special effects. For luck, he carried
a wallet photo of himself grinning in a tiger pit,
fallen unscathed, his crotch above the pit stake.
He wanted to toughen me up for the world. But
at seventeen I preferred Willard, even if it wasn't on maps.

The shelter would have all-you-can-eat ice cream,
pizza delivered, a color TV to watch *Laugh-In.*
Guards would play Scrabble. Nurses would take

temperatures & declare us healthy. In Willard
the dead would lie in peace, preparing their souls
for the angels, rather than rising to eat us alive.
The girl with black eyes across the gym on her cot
would be all I could ask for.

Family Theater

Yet another earnest production of WASPs on a couch
with wintergreen stripes & pillows embroidered
with horses. The father in riding pants
organizes martinis, while three grown daughters
in competing black dresses flaunt histories
of family betrayals, bipolar husbands,
downgraded bonds, silver diaphragm cases
now pawned. The audience dozes,
not even a crinkly candy wrapper to rip
through the boredom. Who cares if a lost uncle
returns, followed by calls from the bank?
Who cares if olives spill on the floor,
breaking the heart of the daughter
who crawls to wipe each with a napkin?

What this drama cries out for is my brother at fourteen
entering stage right in ill-fitting blazer & beltless
gray flannels. Sullenly, he sits on a window stool,
revealing his chubby ass crack, & bolt-loads his rifle,
defiant with pimples & cowlick despite wet combing.
Ignoring the sisters' cold stares & the father's stiff-spined
offer of ginger ale, he tips his head patiently & sights
down the barrel to fire offstage. The audience stirs;
the sniper is stealing the show. If only my parents
could see him acting with such confidence.

Gray hands grip the windowsill. In climbs a pool keeper
in a bloody white shirt, then a bare-footed gardener.
Liberated by death, these zombies tackle the father
behind the couch, gutting their patron in private.
The grown daughters shriek & grab pillows for shields.
One throws an olive the gardener catches in his bloody mouth.
The audience roars, black humor better than none.
My brother keeps shooting, recruiting his army
for vengeance. Next time I'll cast him as
a fourteen year old someone could love.

The Flesh Eater

For politics, he repeats Nader's moth-eaten sound bites.
For fashion, he carries a cow-leather briefcase
with a solitary legal pad thunking inside.
For writing, he uses a silver graduation pen
like the one I lost years ago. For transport,
he drives a rusty tan Civic too small for his bulk.
Driving by, he looks like Humpty Dumpty
in a puffy blue jacket grimy from years without cleaning.
His yellow ski hat makes certain relatives suspect
he's closeted gay; he's never mentioned a date.
For Thanksgiving, he takes our father to a country inn
with pewter candlesticks & paintings of pheasants.
They go easy on cranberry sauce & skip pudding.
For entertainment, he doesn't share my zombie obsession.

For love, he listens to oldies on his bedside clock radio.
Why, I'm not certain. He's not really old enough
for oldies. Nor do I ask about *Playboys*
under the bed with fire engine red covers
he's used since childhood. Our mother believed
loud colors might cure him of shyness.
For solace, he walks at the beach in winter,
recalling what she taught us about buffleheads:
they float happily in water that's nearly freezing.
For work, he volunteers at the Unitarian church:
the welcoming committee for lesbians & gays,
the peace committee protesting Bush.
Once he marched in Manhattan, but avoided
the frightening incident with horses & mounted policemen.
Did I mention the social committee with cider & donuts?
For faith, he follows Emerson: it's all in yourself.
For brotherhood, he looks aside with familiar furtive eyes
& asks what I've done with my life.

Reunion

Chowdered man steams in the china tureen,
creamy, lumpy, smelling oddly like dried jockstraps
I hadn't brought home since high school.
One sip would make me a cannibal zombie,
but my mother ladles my bowl full as her family duty.
My father slurps for the whole table to hear.
My brother crumbles bones on his serving.
They've been off diets for years.
My mother asks if I'd fed the dog.
If I'm not mistaken, we'd buried the dog
& planted a lilac. But I say Snoopy wolfed
down the whole can. My brother, always a nag,
says he found dog ticks in his laundry,
as if somehow I was to blame.
I give him the old stare,
sure he's never been laid.
My mother asks if I needed a clean napkin.
My father insists history treated Nixon badly.
My mother mentions her old show, *The Galloping
Gourmet*, & asks how I like her new recipe.
Stirring my bowl I find the prize, a gold
wedding band I'd swear is my own.
I wonder if my ex still has the two cats.
Upstairs, my mother has kept my bureau like a shrine,
one drawer for camp socks she'd sewn
with my name tags, another for my Boy Scout sash
& Little League shirts. My framed Latin prize
from Greenwich Country Day stands on a doily.
She's been preparing me a long time. A little salty
but good with potatoes. A family must nourish its own.

Mother Reanimated

To walk again after ten years in a wheelchair
with stirrups that secured her limp feet.
To pee not in her diaper, but in toilets of her own choosing.
To spit out her straw & eat with her hands.
To tell the hoarse crone in the next bed to shut up.
To frighten nurses out in the hallway
with her new powers. To press the *down* button
for the first time in years. To knock over plastic flowers
in the lobby where automatic doors release her
stiff legged & determined into sunshine.

The bronze lawn saint, blessing his circle of mulch,
ignores her. Traffic horns blare as she lurches
past bumpers, a mad woman in a blue bathrobe
& sheepskin slippers, deaf to all but the crows.

There's a diner parking lot to cross, a marsh creek
with a half-sunken shopping cart to avoid,
then railroad tracks smelling of creosote ties
that lead her past a brick factory redone as condos.
In her day the factory made Electrolux vacuums.
She gravel-slides down the track embankment
toward the country club tennis courts,
where she won trophies in singles & doubles,
despite early arthritis in her hips. She skirts
the golf course she detested for its manicured lawn.
She saw no need for poisoning dandelions.
Sniffed & trailed by a pedigree collie,
she blunders through hedges into rose gardens,
fragrant but overly trimmed. The fad for koi fish ponds
she doesn't understand. Rounding our garage
she reaches her bushy tomatoes at last,
healthy but poorly staked, marionette plants
needing more twine. In the kitchen drawer,
the same as she left it, she finds string, clippers,
& gloves, then lays the work gloves aside.
To feel dirt under her nails
is all she wanted from Heaven.

Will Nixon grew up in the Connecticut suburbs, lived in Hoboken and Manhattan as a young man, then moved into a Catskills log cabin in 1996. He now lives in Woodstock. His poetry books are *My Late Mother as a Ruffed Grouse* (FootHills Publishing) plus the chapbooks *When I Had It Made* (Pudding House) and *The Fish Are Laughing* (Pavement Saw). His poems have appeared in regional anthologies and dozens of literary journals. His work has been nominated for a Pushcart Prize and listed in *Best American Essays 2004*. His website is willnixon.com.

With Michael Perkins he co-authored *Walking Woodstock: Journeys into the Wild Heart of America's Most Famous Small Town* (Bushwhack Books), which expands upon their columns for the *Woodstock Times*. As an environmental journalist in the past, he was a contributing editor to the *Amicus Journal*, published by the Natural Resources Defense Council, and a special correspondent for the *Adirondack Explorer*. The website for *Walking Woodstock* is BushwhackBooks.com.

For their invaluable help in shaping these poems, Will Nixon thanks the late Saul Bennett, who still lives in these words, Alison Koffler, Nancy Graham, Hope Brennan, Leslie Gerber, Cheryl Rice, Marianna Boncek, and the Hudson Valley poetry community, which has been so supportive for many years. For background information about *Night of the Living Dead*, he consulted the Millennium Edition DVD of the movie plus *The Complete Night of the Living Dead Filmbook* by John Russo.